PATHS, PATIOS
AND PAVING

PATHS, PATIOS AND PAVING

ROGER SWEETINBURGH

WARD LOCK

DEDICATION

This book is dedicated to fond memories of Doreen and her love of gardening.

First published in Great Britain in 1992
by Ward Lock Limited, Villiers House,
41/47 Strand, London WC2N 5JE, England

A Cassell Imprint

© Ward Lock Limited

Text filmset in 11/11½ point ITC Garamond Light
by Columns of Reading
Printed and bound in Great Britain
by Harper-Collins

British Library Cataloguing in Publication Data

Sweetinburgh, Roger
Paths, patios and paving. – (Garden matters)
I. Title   II. Series
712.6

ISBN 0 7063 7049 X

CONTENTS

PREFACE

This book should help anyone who intends to design and build their own patio or garden paths. Patio design, including position, shape and size is dealt with in Chapter 1. In addition to the paving, special features like raised beds, retaining walls and steps etc, are also discussed, with useful advice on their design. In the second chapter, a wide range of paving and walling materials are examined in detail with useful hints aimed at helping you choose the right ones for the right job. One of the most important tasks – to set out and excavate the foundations for paving and walling – is tackled in Chapter 3 along with ideas for surface water drainage. All the operations are described clearly and simply with illustrations to back up the more important points. Chapter 4 goes on to describe how to use concrete and how to build low walls for patio projects, whether they be in brick or stone. These are tackled in the simplest possible terms and are, again, backed up by some useful illustrations. The whole of Chapter 5 is devoted to the laying of paving – concrete slabs, crazy paving, bricks and blocks, and includes hints on cutting and methods of pointing. The final chapter looks at garden paths and all those materials not so far mentioned, including gravel, shingle and bark chippings, together with various types of edging. Throughout the book technical terms have been kept to an absolute minimum and explanations made as simple as possible.

CHAPTER 1

PATIO DESIGN

POSITIONING THE PATIO

Although the ideal position for a patio is often immediately outside patio doors, there may be little point in having the main sitting area here if it receives little or no sun. A walk around the garden several times during a fine day will reveal the sunnier and more sheltered positions which might provide a suitable spot for a patio.

When choosing the best position for a patio, there are several other points to consider: is the site level and, if adjacent to the house, will much soil need excavating? Paving must be at least 150 mm (6 in) below the damp proof course (dpc) and should slope gently away from the house.

Does the garden slope down towards the house, in which case the front edge of the patio is likely to end up below the level of the surrounding ground? Or does the garden have a significant slope away from the house, so that a design will need to incorporate steps down to the rest of the garden?

PATIOS BELOW GROUND LEVEL

These have one or two problems other than the fact that one or more steps will be needed up on to the garden. A retaining wall of some sort (Fig. 1) will have to be

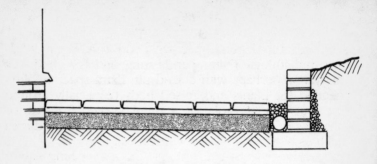

Fig. 1
Patio below ground level with a retaining wall and drainage.

used to keep the garden from falling down on to the patio. A cheaper but more space-consuming alternative is to grade the soil back in the form of a bank, which could then be grassed or turned into a rockery. If the difference in level is significant, quite a few steps may be needed together with a substantial retaining wall or bank. Drainage can also be a problem because all the water is likely to collect and become trapped along the lowest edge. This area will need an efficient drain or gully which, in turn, is connected to some form of outfall, whether it be an existing drain or a soakaway. (Chapter 3).

PATIOS ABOVE GROUND LEVEL

Where the garden is well below the house dpc either the whole or just part of the patio could be raised. In either case, of course, steps will be necessary but a lot more material and construction work will be needed to raise the whole patio. If the drop down to the ground is considerable, some means of preventing people from falling over the edge will be important. This might be a raised bed or some form of balustrade.

PATIO SIZE

The area will depend upon what you want to use it for: just sunbathing, or sitting and eating, and as a children's play area, perhaps with a sand pit. Extra space is often needed for plants and raised beds (especially around the outside), pergola or screens, water features or changes in level and steps. When planning a paved area such as a patio, it is also worth taking into account its practical uses as hard standing for, say, a washing line or small garden buildings.

Do not underestimate the amount of room required for many activities. A sandpit needs plenty of paved space all round it so that any stray sand can be easily cleaned up. A barbecue needs its own allocation of space, which might include fixed seats and work surfaces. A patio which has paving right up to the boundary fences and house walls with no space left for plants can look and feel very harsh. Extra space should be included, particularly around the edges, for a reasonable amount of planting. Beds should be at least 40 cm (16 in) wide. Further space might be needed for raised beds, pots, tubs or even a pond or waterfall.

SHAPING YOUR PATIO

MAKE A SCALE DRAWING

On a piece of card, draw to scale a table, chairs, sun loungers, barbecue and any other feature you want, and cut them out. Make a scale drawing of your intended patio then see if you will be able to fit all your features into it comfortably (Fig. 2). Before you finally decide on the overall shape, get to know the different paving materials available and their limitations, as your choice of materials may restrict the choice of shape.

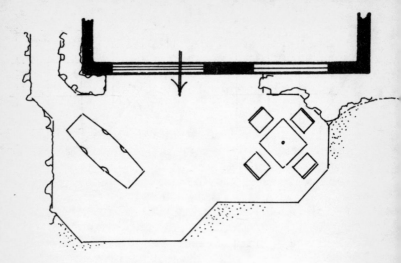

Fig. 2 *Planning a patio for space and use.*

INFLUENCE OF SLAB SHAPES

Curves It is not usually successful to have strongly curved edges to a patio of large square or rectangular slabs. Somewhere along the curved cut edges there are almost certain to be little tiny pieces of slab left perched right on the edge. (Fig. 3a). This can be partly overcome by having a brick edge all around the patio (Fig. 3b). Crazy paving is probably the most flexible when it comes to creating curves. Small units or blocks can also be made to curve or at least be cut to a curve and then be given an edge similar to the brick edging.

Angles A compromise between a simple straight edge and a curved edge is an edge at an angle of, say, 45° (Fig. 4a). This would involve cutting square slabs

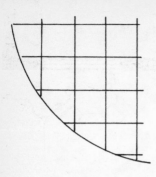 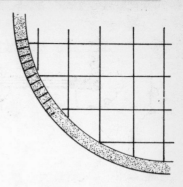

a A curve cut through
   square slabs

b The cut edge finished off
   with brick

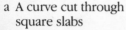

Fig. 3 *Creating a curved patio.*

diagonally in half. Even if the angle was 30°, a brick edging could produce a neat edge.

Hexagonal slabs These can produce a very random shaped patio or, with the help of half slabs, one with straight or angled edges (Fig. 4b).

SHAPING SUNKEN PATIOS

Where a patio cuts into a sloping garden, thus ending up below ground level, complications can arise if the patio reaches considerably further into the slope at one point than it does at another. Those parts of the patio reaching furthest will end up deepest under ground. This usually means that any retaining wall around the edges has to step up and down to compensate. In such circumstances it is probably sensible to limit the degree to which the patio goes in and out and to keep the retaining wall height the same all round, adjusting the garden levels up or down as necessary.

11

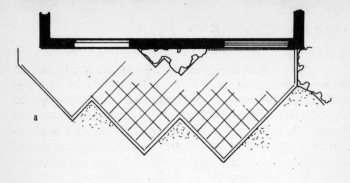

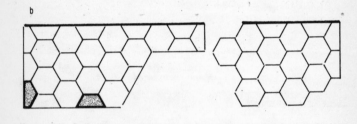

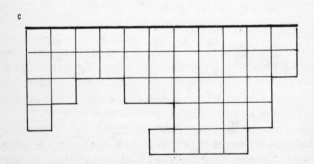

Fig. 4 *Creating an angular patio.*
a A patio angled to 45°.
b Different ways of using hexagonal slabs.
c Stepping in and out using square slabs.

ANGLING THE WHOLE PATIO

It might be, in some circumstances, that square or rectangular slabs look better laid at an angle to the house rather than at 90° to it. This would help to redirect all the views from the house and encourage an angled vista across the garden, perhaps across to one corner. In turn, it would probably mean that features within the patio and the shape of the patio itself would have to be angled too. Some people find it irritating not to be directly facing the sun when sun bathing: this may indicate that the patio has to be shaped and angled to ensure that deck chairs can easily be orientated to face the sun for as long as possible. An alternative to angling is stepping in and out at 90°. This can produce an interesting and attractive layout but does, inevitably, mean a lot of straight lines (Fig. 4c).

RAISED BEDS

Since these are to provide a home for plants they must be free draining and have sufficient depth of soil. A raised bed built directly on top of existing paving with a depth of only about 30 cm (12 in) could soon either fill up with water or become bone dry, thus limiting the choice of plants. Narrow troughs, perhaps only 230 mm (9 in) wide, are equally restricting and usually end up accommodating no more than the usual aubrieta, crocuses, and small annuals. Such shallow or narrow beds, although not ideal, may be the only option in certain designs. In this case, a depth of only 30 cm (12 in) can be made more useful by having some large holes in the base of the raised bed connecting through to the soil below. These then ensure that there is a two-way movement of moisture.

Generally, raised beds should have walls which are at least one brick – 230 mm (9 in) – thick. These would

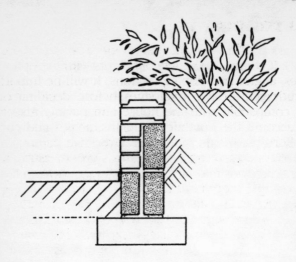

Fig. 5 *A retaining wall 230 mm (9 in) thick using a combination of stock brick and concrete blocks adjacent to the paving.*

then resist any freezing and thawing which might take place inside the beds although in milder districts where frost is rare, thinner walls will be adequate. In addition, the walls of raised beds, if built to an appropriate height, can double up as seating, especially in a barbecue area. Retaining walls in other parts of the patio which have to hold back a considerable weight of soil or materials ought always to be 230 mm (9 in) thick.

Raised beds should be shaped to fit exactly into the paving pattern in order to avoid unnecessary cutting (unless crazy paving is being used).

If expensive materials are being used for the construction of retaining walls, the inner skin could be of something cheaper, like concrete blocks. Care will be needed to ensure that these cheaper materials are not visible when the job is finished (Fig. 5).

BALUSTRADING

This is usually available in stone (or reconstituted stone). It comes in a variety of heights with the option of curves, angles and sloping sections. It will be important to study one or two catalogues before deciding on a style compatible with the house and paving. Also take into account the number of lengths, angles and curves on offer; this will help to avoid excessive cutting.

Where balustrading is used as a safety measure, steel reinforcing rods may have to be brought up from below the paving or from within retaining walls in order to strengthen it. An alternative would be wrought iron railings. These will need to be fixed into fairly deep holes or housings in the retaining walls or paving.

STEPS

Most patios require only a few steps to cope with a change of level. It is therefore easy to work out the height of these and the materials needed. However, where the patio is raised high above the garden, a more extensive flight of steps will be necessary. The two main parts of a step are called the 'tread' (which your foot rests on) and the 'riser'.

To work out the size and number of risers, first measure the precise height to be covered. A comfortable riser is about 15 cm (6 in) so the first calculation is to find out how many times this (or a similar suitable measure) will fit into the overall height. The answer is unlikely to work out exactly. If, for example, it works out to ten whole risers with 8 cm left over, the 8 cm can be shared out over the ten risers (giving 8 mm to each riser) so that ten risers will fit the height exactly.

Once the number (and size) of risers have been worked out, a tread needs to be calculated. A reasonable tread would be about 35 cm (14 in). A flight of steps would therefore have to travel a total distance of 3.5 m (over 11 ft). This is a long distance in a small garden. The most likely solution is often to run the steps down sideways across the front face of the patio or to begin the steps close by the house and run them down the side of the patio. It is vital to work through all these variations and plan carefully before any construction work begins.

How wide should steps be? Very often a significant flight of steps will have a profound effect on the overall design of the patio. There is always a tendency to make a flight of steps too narrow. Unlike a flight of stairs in a house, garden steps often do not have any form of banister, so it is important that they should feel safe to walk down.

Where a flight of steps comes straight off the front of a patio (parallel to the house) the best effect comes from

Fig. 6 *A pergola over a patio could provide both shade and privacy.*

a very wide flight, preferably exactly opposite a key window or door. Where the garden slopes steeply away from the house, this arrangement gives the best opportunity for some sort of view into the lower part of the garden. Low walls or raised beds around such a patio would have the opposite effect, shutting out the rest of the garden.

PERGOLAS

Positioned over part of the patio a pergola (Fig. 6) will provide some shade and possibly some screening from neighbouring upstairs windows. It could also have the disadvantage of making some of the rooms in the house rather dark.

On large patios, vertical supports could be built from brick or stone, but on a smaller scale, wooden uprights would be more appropriate. Pressure-treated sawn timber is more suitable than rustic poles on a patio and the structure should be at least 2.1 m (7 ft) high so that climbing plants do not obstruct movement. These uprights could be slotted into metal sockets which have been concreted into the patio surface, but a tight fit is essential if the pergola is to be completely stable.

A pergola will be enhanced by the addition of climbing plants, and a good deep planting space will need to be allowed for if they are to succeed.

CHOOSING A WATER FEATURE

Unless the patio is quite large, any water feature will have to be relatively small. If there is the probability of young children playing on the patio, the feature will have to be childproof.

Raised ponds A raised pond, like a raised bed, will need brick or block walls at least 230 mm (9 in) thick to

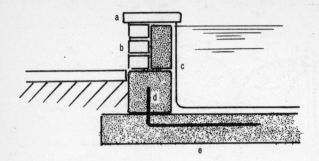

Fig. 7 *Construction of a raised pool within a patio.*
a Coping b Brickwork c Rendering d Steel
reinforcing into concrete blocks   e Steel-reinforced
concrete.

withstand possible freezing and thawing. In general, it
does not want to be more than about 400 mm (16 in)
above the patio surface, preferably a little less than this.
In some cases, this may not give sufficient depth of
water, so the base of the pond might have to be below
the patio surface. (Fig. 7).

The most appropriate foundation would be a steel-
reinforced slab or raft of concrete about 150 mm (6 in)
thick upon which the walls could be built. These walls
would need some form of coping (which might double
up as a seat) and the inside of the pool will have to be
rendered with a mixture of washed sharp sand and
cement. (Chapter 4).

Submerged ponds An off the peg pool can be
bought as moulded fibreglass or be a water tank of the
type normally used inside houses. Patio ponds which
are flush with the patio surface are built in a similar way
to raised ponds but it must be remembered that these
are more dangerous for children.

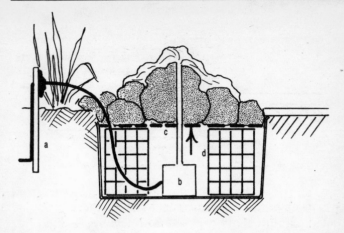

Fig. 8 *Construction of a small foundation ideal for patios.*
a Electricity supply   b Submersible pump   c Strong
grid to support rocks   d Polypropylene crates to
support grid.

Fountains or cascades These additional features
must not be so vigorous that, on a windy day, the water
blows all over the patio paving. A bubble fountain or a
foam jet might be more appropriate. Ponds on two
levels with a cascade from one to the other can make a
very effective patio feature but will require more space.
Alternatively, water could be made to pour out of a patio
wall and down into a small pool below. There are a
number of water features, notably mill stones and large
rocks (Fig. 8), where water is pumped up through the
centre and encouraged to flow down over the sides into
an area of pebbles or cobbles. There is no visible depth
of water – a large reservoir is situated beneath the
millstone or rocks. A feature like this is obviously
relatively safe, even with young children around.

Submersible pumps An electric pump has to be

situated in the main reservoir of water and will require a power source. All the electricity cables and connections will have to be planned at the beginning because some of these may have to pass through or beneath walls and paving. Armoured cable and special weatherproof sockets should be used and connected to an earthed trip circuit in the house. A qualified electrician must be used for this work.

LIGHTS

There are several types of lighting available. Apart from full floodlighting, which is usually white and run on full voltage, all the other types – low level spot lights or uplighters – can be high or low voltage, white or coloured. A pergola is the ideal place for spot lights or down lighting. Planted borders and raised beds can look very effective with white or coloured lighting and, of course, a water feature lends itself to different lighting effects. The area around a barbecue and steps will need special attention for obvious reasons.

IRRIGATION SYSTEMS

A number of systems exist which allow raised beds, pots, tubs and any other planted areas to be watered automatically. Most are based on the idea of trickle nozzles fixed into long, thin, flexible tubes or very thin 'spaghetti' lines which deliver a prolonged, slow trickle of water. Liquid fertilizer can be added at source and results are usually quite spectacular, especially on hot sunny patios where the plants end up receiving generous amounts of everything they need.

CHAPTER 2

MATERIALS

PAVING

Many types of material are available for paving, some more suited to certain situations than others. They range from the very soft sandstones through to hard, smooth slate and marble, and from bricks or concrete slabs to timber decking.

NATURAL STONE

Sandstone is usually an attractive pale brown or honey colour but, being very soft, is not generally suitable in persistently wet localities. Because it absorbs water, it can become mossy, perhaps slippery. Frost will freeze any water in the stone and, on thawing, will often break it up. Under relatively dry, frost-free conditions, this type of stone will survive for many years, but may wear away under intense foot traffic.

Other types of stone are available, many of which are quite hard and ideal for paving. Colour varies enormously from creamy white, grey through to dark brown. The best are those which have a reasonably even thickness and a slightly textured or non-slip surface. The supplier should be able to advise on their suitability for different situations.

Stone is sometimes sold in random rectangular pieces (Fig. 9a) and can be put together as a random

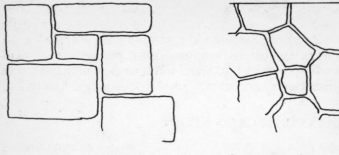

a Random rectangular paving

b Crazy paving

Fig. 9 *Different types of paving.*

rectangular pattern. Other stones come in totally random mixed shapes (Fig. 9b) and sizes and is therefore ideal for crazy paving. It does help to sort out a stock of pieces with good straight edges or with a particular curve so that these can be used as edging pieces – much as you might before beginning a jigsaw puzzle. There are also more specialized stones to consider:

Slate and marble These may have to be cut to fit certain shapes and, since both slate and marble are so hard this will need special equipment. Generally these two stones are not ideal in wet conditions because they can become slippery; they tend to be used more in countries which have predominantly dry conditions.

Setts or cobbles Cube-shaped pieces of stone (usually granite) are available, generally grey but sometimes in pink. Because they are very hard, they are especially good for driveways and kerbs, but they are often too uneven for general patio use.

Round cobbles (or beach stones) Because they result in such an uneven surface, cobbles are not really suitable for general patio paving but can be used as an interesting feature within a patio, perhaps as a small patch upon which to stand a tub or pot. In some street schemes they are actually used to discourage foot traffic.

RECONSTITUTED STONE

In an attempt to make concrete slabs look as natural as possible, a high proportion of natural stone is sometimes incorporated in their manufacture. They are called reconstituted stone slabs. They offer the advantages of a natural looking product with the precision of a concrete slab so that a precise yet natural-looking surface can be achieved. The colour of the slab will be influenced by the type of stone used – there are many colours and shades available. Most have a non-slip, slightly roughened surface but there are some which have been polished. These may become slippery under certain circumstances but the polishing does reveal the natural stone and produces a very attractive finish. Most of the unpolished reconstituted slabs have a reasonably natural or mellow appearance making them ideally suited to be used in conjunction with brick paving.

BRICKS AND BLOCK PAVIORS

Only certain types of bricks are suitable for paving. These must be highly frost resistant and, as such, are likely to be classed as 'stock' or possibly 'engineering' bricks. Stock bricks are available in a wide selection of colours and shades and, in general, have a slightly rough surface. Engineering bricks, although very hard and frost resistant, are very often smooth, even shiny and could become slippery. House flettons are usually unsuitable in frosty situations.

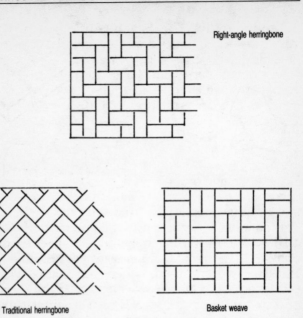

Right-angle herringbone

Traditional herringbone

Basket weave

Fig. 10 *Types of brick paving.*

Creating patterns with bricks In most cases, bricks are laid 'frog' down. Because the majority are produced for use in walls, their standard size means that when laid frog down, two widths add up to just less than one whole length. In certain paving patterns, especially basket weave and herringbone (Fig. 10), this will mean that small joints will be left between bricks which will need pointing. In recent years, special brick and concrete paviors have been introduced which have a length exactly equal to two widths. This therefore means that all paving patterns can be achieved without the need for pointing. These paviors vary in thickness – anything from 65 mm (2½ in) down to about 50 mm

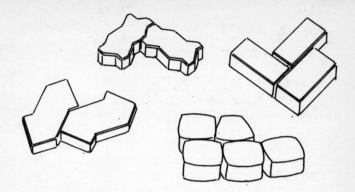

Fig. 11 *Different shaped concrete paviors.*

(2 in) depending on the make, style and material.

While conventional bricks are usually laid individually on mortar and pointed up afterwards, brick paviors are laid out on a bed of sharp sand and vibrated down into position with a special machine. This vibration cannot take place unless a strong kerb or edging has been fixed all around the area first. Without this, the paviors move all over the place when the machine is used.

Concrete block paviors   There is an extensive range of different shaped and coloured concrete block paviors available (Fig. 11); some are perhaps more usually associated with shopping precincts rather than garden patios. Concrete block paviors can also be used to produce a strong and attractive kerb for a wide range of driveway materials. Others have been designed for the creation of circular patterns. These are particularly useful for winding or curved paths as well as for circular patios or even semi-circular steps. There is slightly less choice available in the colour and shape of brick paviors although a number of interesting shapes have been developed. The overall effect of brick tends to be more mellow and 'natural' than it is with concrete paviors.

CONCRETE SLABS

There are three main types of concrete slab available:

Hydraulically pressed slabs Although the standard 'industrial' version tends to be in grey concrete with pimples on both sides (small ones on the upper surface, larger ones beneath) there are quite a few more attractive types available. Some have a non-slip surface while others are polished and contain attractive stones. Those which measure 60 cm (24 in) square or larger are very heavy to lay but the more ornamental types are often smaller and will produce a very durable area of paving. These slabs tend to cost more than vibrated or wet moulded slabs. Since they usually have very precise, often perfectly square edges, they can be laid butt jointed', i.e. without pointed joints.

Vibrated slabs These are often only 35–40 mm (1½–1¾ in) thick and rather weak compared with hydraulically pressed slabs. However, laid on an adequate base, they are ideal for patios and domestic paths. They nearly always have a non-slip surface and are available in a wide range of sizes and colours. They are reasonably light and accurate to work with but usually look best with pointed joints. Cutting is quite easy because they are not very dense.

Wet moulded slabs These are produced by pouring concrete into a mould. The mould often has some form of patterning which is obviously transferred on to the upper surface of the slab. This technique gives rise to an enormous range of styles; mock cobbles and sets, imitation stone, even imitation crazy paving. There is an equally wide choice of colours – from natural stone through to pink, green etc. Some are produced with a perfectly smooth surface on one side and a 'combed' or

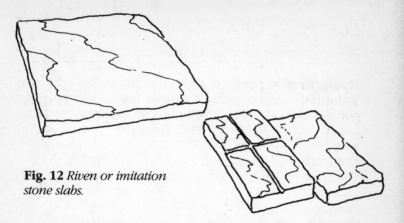

Fig. 12 *Riven or imitation stone slabs.*

'brushed' finish on the other. Although they may look better with the smooth side uppermost, this can become slippery and some people prefer the rough side up for safety. Unfortunately, this can look rather ugly. It is probably better to use a slab which has an attractively textured or riven surface (Fig. 12) which will be relatively non-slip. Many of these slabs have bevelled or sloping edges (which facilitate their extraction from the mould) and where these are laid smooth side up they can be butt jointed to leave a thin, pointed or unpointed join. If, however, they are laid the other way up or have a square or rustic edge, proper joints and pointing certainly enhance the overall effect.

Moulded slabs are not very strong and are not always very precise. I can remember working on one patio using 60 cm (24 in) square moulded slabs and having quite a struggle making all the corners come together properly. There always seemed to be one which would stick up above the others, usually because some of the slabs were very slightly twisted. Trying to knock the corners down only resulted in breakages. It is worth mentioning that these slabs were quite inexpensive.

Some makes of slabs come in several different sizes,

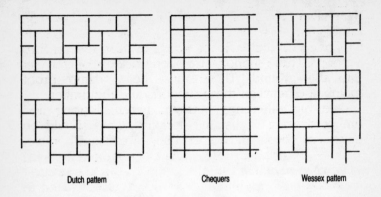

Dutch pattern   Chequers   Wessex pattern

Fig. 13 *Slab paving patterns.*

making various patterns possible (Fig. 13). Hexagonal slabs are a little unusual in that they have two types of half slab which can be used to produce straight edges.

CERAMIC TILES

These are not used as extensively as the other types of paving units, but they do produce a unique and very attractive surface with a wide selection of colours and embossed patterns. Care has to be taken to use only frost resistant tiles and that their surface is non-slip. They are usually laid on a concrete base just as they might be laid on a floor in the house but, like all outdoor paving, particular attention has to be paid to surface drainage and falls.

TIMBER DECKING

The best timbers are hardwoods because they are both durable and fine grained (less likely to splinter). Pressure-treated softwood is thought by some to be just as durable and, providing it is planed (smooth) rather than sawn (rough) it is a useful alternative. Decking, rather like any other form of timber flooring, is supported on timber joists which, in turn, rest on firm supports. These supports are often brick or concrete set into the ground. There must be a damp proof membrane between these supports and the timber.

One big difference between house flooring and timber decking is that the decking planks should be given a gap between each to allow for expansion in wet weather. Something in the order of 6–10 mm (½–¾ in) is usually sufficient, so that even under the wettest conditions, a gap remains to allow surface water to escape. Failure to do this results in a watertight surface which becomes very slippery and dangerous.

If hardwood is used, then a suitable timber treatment should be painted on to enhance its durability and appearance. If untreated soft wood is used it must be thoroughly painted (or sprayed) with a weather-resistant, wide-spectrum preservative. This may or may not be coloured. If it is colourless, then a stain will probably be needed afterwards. Pressure-treated softwood will need only a stain to provide the right colour. Planks are usually nailed rather than screwed although high quality hardwood decking can be fixed with brass screws which are either countersunk or have their heads protected by screw cups. Timberwork can be further extended into steps, handrails, small bridges and so on.

WALLING

NATURAL STONE

There are as many different types of stone available for walling as there are for paving. Many are the same – just mined or quarried in a different way. Most stone garden walls are mortared and need a stable, perhaps concrete foundation.

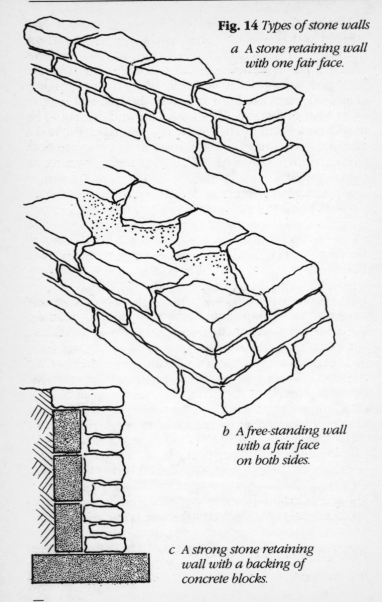

Fig. 14 *Types of stone walls*

a A stone retaining wall with one fair face.

b A free-standing wall with a fair face on both sides.

c A strong stone retaining wall with a backing of concrete blocks.

Ideally, the stone wall would have one smooth 'fair' face. In order to achieve this, it will have to be at least as thick as the largest stones. Lining up all the front faces of the stone to achieve the fair face will mean that the back face will be left completely uneven and unsightly (Fig. 14a). For a fair front and back, the wall will have to be at least two stones thick (Fig. 14b) and this could be as much as 40 cm (16 in). Stone is often expensive and a cheaper alternative if the wall must have a fair face both sides together with strength, is it have a backing of concrete blocks (Fig. 14c). Near the top of the wall it will probably be necessary to have stone front and back just to finish it off, even if this just means a stone coping. Smaller stone retaining walls need not be so substantial and can, therefore, be without a concrete block backing. Soil will hide the uneven reverse side of these walls.

Dry stone walls   These have no mortar or concrete foundations and are quite commonly used as retaining walls against banks or for raised beds. They should lean back slightly (have a 'batter') but not be stepped back. This batter will increase their stability. Free-standing stone walls, often used to keep sheep at bay on hill farms, may need to start as thick as 1 m (3 ft) at their base and taper gradually towards the top. This extra thickness is also necessary in order to achieve a fair face on both sides. Any voids within the wall are filled with rubble and small stones. A coping of flattish stones set vertically on their side is often used to finish the wall off. It is essential that all stone walls are built with as good a bond as possible between the stones and to avoid excessively long vertical joints (page 61).

RECONSTITUTED STONE

Just as there is for paving, so there are reconstituted

stone products available for walling. These take on the general appearance of the stone they incorporate but are obviously more precise in shape than the real thing. Some are used as a kit of different sizes for a random effect; others are one standard size. The latter will produce a very predictable looking wall with brick like jointing, but the overall effect is more mellow. One advantage of the reconstituted random walling is that it comes as a standard thickness with a smooth back face. This has the effect of producing two fair faces – one in stone, the other in stone-like concrete.

BRICK

All brick garden walls, like brick paving, are highly susceptible to frost damage, so stock or engineering bricks should be used wherever possible. Even though the bricks in a wall might be frost resistant, a damp proof course of some sort is still advisable, especially if the wall is free standing. The ideal damp proof course is a couple of courses of engineering bricks positioned a little above ground level and, ideally, another course used as a coping on top (Fig. 15a).

Walls which are used to retain soil may not have a horizontal dpc but can be painted (tanked) with a bitumastic compound on the side against which soil will be stacked. This, while not giving total protection against damp, will help to prolong the life of the bricks.

All brick walls should have concrete foundation (Chapters 3 and 4).

Brick retaining walls These are usually double skinned – the front of brick and the back of 100 mm (4 in) thick concrete blocks giving a total thickness of 230 mm (9 in). The top few courses, including some form of coping or 'soldier' course, should be all brick so that the concrete blocks are not visible. Weep holes will

a Engineering bricks used as a coping and dpc

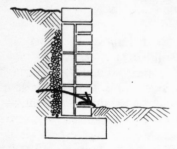

b A brick and block retaining wall with aggregate behind for drainage and a weephole for through drainage.

Fig. 15 *Construction of brick walls.*

be needed to allow the passage of excess water (Fig. 15b).

Free-standing walls Where walls are free standing yet still 230 mm (9 in) thick, they would be all brick and referred to as whole brick walls. Walls of half this thickness are referred to as half brick walls, but are obviously less strong, and in most circumstances, benefit from the addition of piers at intervals along their length.

Brick bonds (Fig 16) Bricks in a half brick wall are laid to a pattern called stretcher bond. Whole brick walls can be achieved by having two half brick stretcher bond walls built back to back, but tied together with steel ties. Alternatively, whole brick walls use a number of other

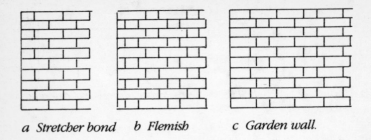

a Stretcher bond   *b Flemish*   *c Garden wall.*

Fig. 16 *Types of brick bonds.*

bonds, where bricks are laid both longways and across the wall in order to achieve solid strength. These bonds do require a little more effort and often involve some cutting of bricks and, in general, are perhaps more applicable to large garden walls rather than the smaller types dealt with in this book.

Coping/capping (Fig 17) All brick walls should be protected by coping or capping. The simplest is a soldier course (bricks laid on their sides) of, if possible, engineering bricks but at the very least, stock bricks. More elaborate copings can be made by the inclusion of tiles, usually called creasing tiles. Alternatively a course or two of bricks could be stepped out (corbelled) to produce an overhang, commonly seen on chimneys.

CONCRETE BLOCKS

These are usually cheaper than most other walling materials, and are not very attractive. Two thicknesses are commonly available – 100 mm (4 in) and 230 mm (9 in), although sometimes 150 mm (6 in) can be found. The most common way of making at least one side more attractive is to have a brick coping and to render the visible face or faces of the wall with sharp sand and

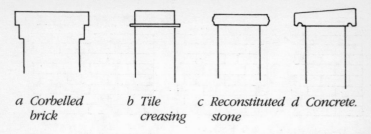

a Corbelled brick   *b Tile creasing*   *c Reconstituted stone*   *d Concrete.*

Fig. 17 *Types of wall copings.*

cement. This can then be decorated with exterior wall paint.

SCREEN BLOCKS

Made in a mould, these are rather brittle so must be handled with care. Sometimes referred to as pierced screen blocks, they are available in various patterns which, when fitted together, produce an overall, repeating pattern. They are not bonded or overlapped – all the joints run in lines – so they need strengthening with piers at reasonably frequent intervals. Special blocks, called pilaster blocks, are manufactured for use in constructing these piers, but a more attractive wall can be produced using bricks or stone for the piers and by having some brick or stone work running all along the base of the wall. Concrete copings are made for the top of the wall but, again, a brick (or stone) coping could be used so that the wall ends up with large panels of screen blocks being completely framed in brick or stone (Fig. 18)

TERRACOTTA TILES

Shaped and profiled these can also form screen walling. When fitted together they produce a three dimensional

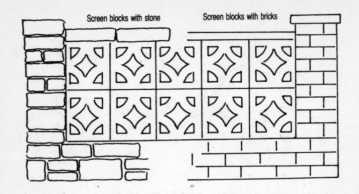

Screen blocks with stone   Screen blocks with bricks

Fig. 18 *A wall using screen blocks.*

'see-through' wall but are not usually capable of producing a wall entirely on their own. They nearly all require a brick or stone base, piers and coping so that they, once again, end up as a panel within a more substantial wall.

Unlike the concrete screen blocks, which are usually white, most terracotta profiled tiles are red, brown or occasionally dark grey. Their design seldom allows much room for the mortar which has to hold them together, so construction is fiddly and care is needed to avoid staining the tiles with excess mortar. A similar panel can be made from the clay ridge tiles normally used for the ridge of a house roof. These can be fixed on top of one another in a staggered fashion to produce a series of half-moon-shaped holes (Fig. 19).

Generally speaking, the terracotta products produce a wall which is more attractive, mellow and traditional than is possible from concrete screen blocks. However, concrete blocks are more substantial, require less help from brick or stone and are therefore likely to produce a cheaper 'see-through' wall.

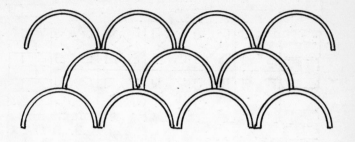

Fig. 19 *Clay ridge tiles used as a panel within a brick wall.*

TIMBER

Most vertical timber structures would be classed as screens or fences and are not therefore covered by this book. Railway sleepers, however, along with very thick poles, can be fixed together to produce retaining walls.

Railway sleepers laid flat side down, on top of one another with the joints staggered for extra strength, make a useful low wall. They do need to be fixed to prevent the soil from pushing them out, and there is a number of ways this can be done. They can be drilled so that the holes line up and run right down from top to bottom. Steel rods can then be pushed through and hammered down into the ground below. Alternatively, some form of battening can be fixed at the back but the timber used for this must have been pressure treated. Where sleepers are laid flat to retain a bank, some half-length sleepers can be run back into the bank for extra stability. Only the end of these would be visible from the front.

Taller walls can be achieved by setting sleepers or thick poles vertically into the ground (Fig. 20). Obviously,

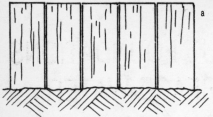

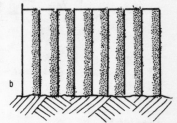

Fig. 20 *Types of wooden walls.*
a A low wall of sleepers
b A low wall of vertical
*   poles.*

the amount which needs to go into the ground will
depend upon the degree of stability required, but a
good depth – perhaps 60 cm (24 in) will be necessary
for a retaining wall 1.2 m (4 ft) high. Where soil is very
stable, concrete should not be necessary. Some form of
cross battening at the back is a good idea near the top of
a retaining wall to prevent individual sleepers from
being pushed out of line.

CHAPTER 3

SETTING OUT FOUNDATIONS AND SURFACE WATER DRAINAGE

A foundation is the most important part of any wall or area of paving. Apart from needing to be the right size and shape, it will have to be strong enough for the job and at exactly the right level in the ground.

> ### Useful tools
>
> spade/fork
> club hammer + pegs
> string lines
> measuring tape
> corner square, wooden or metal
> spirit level
> straight edge

WALL FOUNDATIONS

If the wall is to be mortared it will need a concrete foundation. This should be twice the width of the wall upon it so that the concrete protrudes by half the wall width down either side and at either end. It will be a strip foundation and must always be perfectly level.

Wherever possible, a concrete foundation must be based on firm ground (subsoil), and in some districts this could be quite close to the surface. Where the topsoil is particularly deep and soft, the foundation may have to be set quite deep down. This does not necessarily mean that the concrete will have to be any thicker. Any wall that begins well below ground level can start with concrete blocks. Not until these almost reach the surface do the more ornamental materials – bricks, stone – have to be used. This can save quite a lot of money.

If the wall is not going to be very large and the ground is very soft, an alternative to digging deep is to set the foundation a little way down but run steel reinforcing rods the entire length of the concrete. This should prevent any cracking from taking place in such soft ground. Larger walls might need concrete piles under these conditions, but the technique is not covered in this book.

Where paving is to be brought right up to the wall, the concrete foundation must be deep enough to allow the paving to be laid over the top, otherwise concrete may have to be laboriously chipped away to make room for the paving.

PAVING FOUNDATIONS

There are two aspects to setting out paving – its shape and its levels.

SHAPE

It helps if a complex area of paving is drawn to scale on paper. By using the right scale, all the measurements can be taken off the drawing and transferred to the ground. Where circles are involved, it will help to know exactly where the centres should be in relation to an existing building or some other feature, so that they can be redrawn on the ground.

If walls have been planned around the edges of the paving, especially if this paving is to be units of a specific size and shape, then setting out will have to be done particularly carefully. The bottom portion of these walls will be built before the paving is laid, so if the setting out is wrong, slabs may need extra cutting or unforeseen gaps filling in with gravel.

Once the shape of the paved area has been marked out, all the soft topsoil should be removed – down as far as firm ground if possible. The excavation should extend a little beyond the eventual paved area and be given the same slope or 'falls' as the finished job.

FALLS

The degree of fall varies with the type of paving and how rapidly rain water is likely to drain from its surface. An average fall would be 1 cm per metre (1:100). Very smooth paving could have slightly less and rough paving (brick or stone) slightly more. Some thought must be given to how these falls are going to affect the paving's relationship with the surrounding ground or features. Over a long distance 1 cm per metre can build up to quite a substantial drop. Sometimes it is worth splitting the direction of fall so that the paving slopes in two directions, thus reducing the amount of drop in any one place.

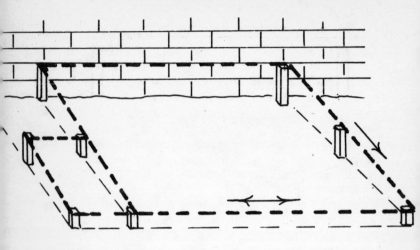

Fig. 21 *Setting out a patio with pegs and string.*

Using pegs Wooden pegs, perhaps 25 mm (1 in) square will be useful in predicting exactly where the surface of the finished paving will end up (Fig. 21). When most of the excavation has been carried out there will be at least one location within the area of paving where it is easy to decide exactly where its surface will have to be. This could be a certain distance below the damp proof course on an adjacent building, or it might be flush with some existing paving or a lawn.

The first peg should be banged in until its top is level with this one certain point. If the proposed paving is to be level in one direction, then further pegs can mark the same level as this first one. This can be easily achieved with the use of a straight edge and spirit level.

Progressing from here, other pegs can then be put in

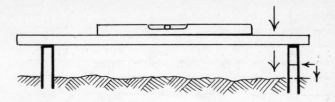

a Setting a fall using a mark on a peg

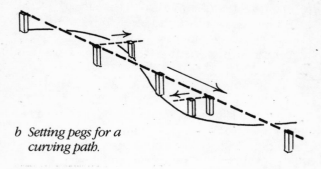

*b Setting pegs for a
   curving path.*

Fig. 22 *Creating a fall to drain surface water*

to indicate the appropriate rise or fall. One way of doing
this is to make two pegs level using the straight edge
and spirit level. A small mark is then drawn on the pegs
at what is to be the lower level, exactly level with the
ground at that point. Depending on its distance from the
neighbouring peg, a second is then drawn on it, the
appropriate amount above the first (Fig. 22a). If, for
example, these two pegs are 2 m apart, the second mark
on the peg will have to be 2 cm above the one denoting
ground level; if the distance between the two pegs is
3 m, the second mark will be 3 cm above the first. The
peg with the marks is then knocked in until the higher
mark is level with the ground – the peg will be lower by
the right amount for a fall of 1:100.

WINDING PATHS

The easiest way to set out levelling pegs for a winding path is to strike a straight line from one end of the proposed route to the other, using a peg at either end (with the tops at the right level for the finished job) and a string stretched really tight between the two (running over the tops). Other pegs can then be inserted at intervals, their tops level with the string.

Where the path bends away from the string, a level can be taken from a peg inserted level with the string at that point and repeated sideways on to the edge of the path. The central string line therefore acts as a constant reference (Fig. 22b).

If there is no appreciable slope from one end of a path to the other, a cross fall can be used. Pegs are inserted down one side only. Other pegs are then put in on the opposite side of the path with a suitable rise or fall so that the path slopes to one side. An alternative is to give the path a camber by having the centre slightly higher – a useful technique for wide paths.

Since the tops of pegs predict the surface of the finished job, a straight edge should be used to check, in all directions, that there are no potential dips or hollows where puddles might eventually form. This is especially important on large areas of paving – patios, driveways etc.

SURFACE WATER DRAINAGE

Having given an area of paving a fall, arrangements have to be made, in most cases, to dispose of the rainwater which will collect at the lowest point. In some situations this water can simply drain into soil which is flush with or slightly below the paving surface. A similar arrangement where paving comes up against grass may also work in light soils but if the soil is clay or the grass is higher than the paving, problems with puddles may occur in very wet weather. Sometimes a narrow, pebble-filled gully will be sufficient but often a more elaborate drainage system is required.

COLLECTING THE WATER

French drains These are gravel- or stone-filled gullies which run along the lowest edge of the paving. Along the bottom beneath the gravel is usually a porous pipe into which the water can pass.

Gully 'pots' These are relatively small chambers, moulded in pottery or plastic (Fig. 23a). They are often about 23 cm (9 in) square (or round) and about 30 cm (12 in) deep, with a removable grille fitted into the top. The bottom of the chamber usually changes into a pipe which has an upturn before leaving horizontally to connect with a pipe system. This forms a trap from which silt and leaves can be collected periodically. In areas of garden paving, relatively inconspicuous gullies can be used although it is often necessary to have more than one, depending on the fall. For driveways, where the volume of water is often greater, slightly larger gullies may be necessary. These usually have steel rather than plastic grilles suitable for wheeled traffic.

Slit gullies Useful for collecting or intercepting water across the bottom of a slope, particularly where there is a danger of water flooding into a garage. Some are U-shaped channels with a grille across the top and a facility at one end to connect with a pipe system. Others are moulded in concrete with a slit all along the top.

Silt traps Most water which drains off paving or driveways carries a good deal of rubbish and silt. Many of the gullies described have their own facility for intercepting and holding on to this rubbish so that it is not passed on to the outfall. Some, notably French drains and slit gullies, have no such facility, which means that special chambers will have to be added to the system for the collection of silt.

These silt traps can be built in brick, concrete or plastic sections. The pipes enter and leave several centimetres up from the bottom so that any rubbish can lodge in this bottom portion (the trap) until it is cleared out (Fig. 23b). These chambers can measure anything from about 30 cm (12 in) square up to 60 cm (24 in) or more, and will be as deep as is necessary. They need some sort of top which can be fitted at or even below ground level. Those below ground level (buried) must have their location recorded so that from time to time they can be retrieved for cleaning. These chambers also provide the opportunity to switch from porous to non-porous pipes and to change direction – pipes should never go round steep bends.

PIPES

The whole system has to be linked with pipes. Some just carry water from A to B and are non-porous, with water-tight joints. Others, as in the case of the French drain, have to be porous in order to gather water.

Once water has been collected, it must be conducted downhill to the outfall. A slope of 1 cm per metre (1:100) is usually sufficient but this does mean that some careful calculation is needed to ensure that the outfall is sufficiently lower than the collection point to allow a good fall. It is also important to realize that much of the drainage system will have to be in place before any walls or paving are built, so some forward planning is essential.

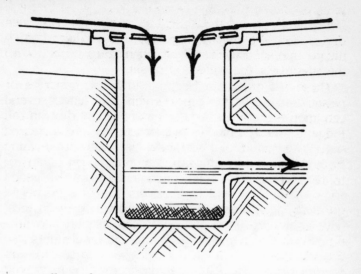

a A gully pot for use in paving

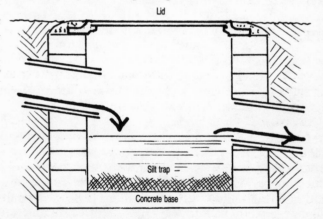

b A brick built silt trap.

Fig. 23 *Two examples of ways of trapping silt from surface water.*

DRAINAGE OUTFALLS

These are places where water can be conducted to by the pipes once it has been collected. The most common outfall is the soakaway.

Hollow soakaway (Fig 24a)   This is an underground chamber at least 5 m (or 15 ft) away from a dwelling (if possible) often formed from concrete blocks or concrete rings. The bottom of the soakaway is usually just soil and the sides should be, in some way, very porous. A strong lid (sometimes reinforced concrete) is obviously needed so that people or vehicles do not fall in. This lid would normally be at least 30 cm (12 in) below ground level with a chimney-like column of brickwork built around a hole in the lid so that access is possible for cleaning out. This chimney is brought up to the garden surface and given a proper steel frame and cover which may need disguising.

This type of soakaway is quite elaborate, may be fairly costly to construct but can hold a good volume of water which is especially valuable in clay or other slow-draining soils. The size of the chamber must, of course, reflect the likely volume of water piped into it or, alternatively, the area of paving to be drained. Many such soakaways are 1.5 m (5 ft) wide, and deep.

Rubble-filled soakaway (Fig. 24b)   Another type of soakaway, basically a hole in the ground filled with hardcore and stones, is easier and cheaper to construct but holds less water. It is, however, usually adequate in fairly well-drained soils or where there is not a need for anything too large. It can be any size but probably not smaller than 1 m (3 ft) in any dimension. Large stones or hardcore go at the bottom and smaller stones near the top. Over these, there would be a sheet of heavy-gauge polythene before a layer of soil. The depth of soil will

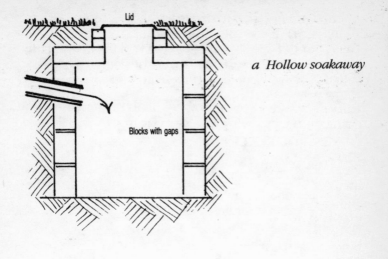

a Hollow soakaway

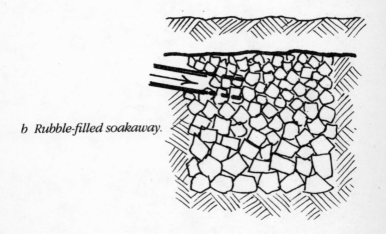

b Rubble-filled soakaway.

Fig. 24 *Two types of soakaways.*

depend upon the nature of garden above. Beneath lawn, 20 cm (8 in) is usually sufficient but at least 40 cm (16 in) would be sensible in an area of regularly cultivated soil. There is a danger, of course, that this type of soakaway could become silted up in time.

ALTERNATIVE FORMS OF OUTFALL

streams
ditches
ponds (with an overflow)
existing drains, but not foul
    water drains (sewage
    systems).

CHAPTER 4

FOUNDATIONS AND WALLS

MIXING AND PLACING CONCRETE

From now on, quite a selection of tools and materials are required and good organization will help to speed up work and make the job easier.

Before beginning work it pays to get all tools and ingredients together on site, and to have a clear idea of the order in which work is going to proceed.

**EQUIPMENT FOR LAYING
THE FOUNDATIONS
OF A WALL**

cement ⎫
ballast ⎬ for concrete
water supply ⎭ (see below)
large board for mixing
wooden float
polythene to protect drying concrete
shovel and barrow

CONCRETE

Three ingredients are needed for concrete: cement, all-in ballast and water.

Cement Usually purchased in 50 kg bags. Portland cement is the type normally used but if concrete foundations are to be laid in excessively wet conditions – even where there is running water, high alumina cement can be used. This sets very rapidly but is not quite as strong as Portland cement in the long term. With the type of work we are concerned with here, this question of strength is unlikely to be a problem. Bags of cement must be kept dry. Cement has a limited shelf life, and, if bought from a place where the turnover is slow, may be rather old. Fresh cement is often warm and the bags are relatively soft.

All-in ballast This is a controlled mix of stones and sand. It can be bought by weight or volume, most commonly in cubic metres.

Water The easiest way to have water constantly available is to run a hose pipe into a large dustbin so that this is kept full. Water can then be taken out in bucketfuls. The water used must be clean.

MIXING CEMENT

An average mix is by volume: 1 part of cement to, say, 6 parts of ballast. The ingredients are mixed dry on a large board or concrete surface and the water is added to a hollow made in the centre of the dry mixture. This mixture is then systematically and thoroughly turned with more water being added until the mixture is evenly wetted to the point where it is soft but not so runny that it would pour like a liquid.

PLACING THE CONCRETE

It is useful to have thin pegs protruding from the excavation with their tops indicating the level of the

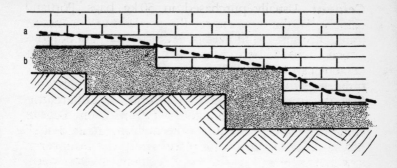

Fig. 25 *A stepped foundation for a wall in sloping ground.*
a Ground level
b Concrete foundation.

finished concrete. Concrete can be placed all around these so that they end up just visible on the surface.

The concrete should then be tamped into position. This is done by banging it with a block of wood or a wooden float until, gradually, a wettish 'fatty' surface appears. If the mix is too wet, it will be like banging a jelly. A mixture which is too dry will not produce a fatty surface. Although a very wet mix does, conveniently, find its own level it does not end up as strong as a slightly stiffer mix.

Thin pegs need not be removed but pegs thicker than about 4 cm (1½ in) should be taken out and extra concrete added while it is still wet just in case the presence of these thicker pegs weakens the foundation.

All wall foundations must be level. If the ground slopes significantly, a foundation can be stepped up or down to compensate (Fig. 25). A step must equal exactly one or more courses of brick or blockwork so that subsequent courses passing across the point where a step occurs can do so smoothly.

CURING

Concrete must be allowed to set or cure gradually and not be allowed to dry out too quickly so that it can reach full strength. A covering of polythene will help by preventing the rapid loss of moisture. Low temperatures may also inhibit setting and a special antifreeze additive will be necessary in very cold weather. Once set, the concrete foundation must be kept clean before bricks, blocks or stone are laid.

MORTAR MIXES

Most walls and areas of paving require mortar of one sort or another. This will be made from soft sand, cement, water and lime. The lime acts as a plasticizer, making the mix smoother and easier to use. An alternative to lime is a proprietary plasticizer which can be added during mixing.

PROPORTIONS FOR MORTAR IN WALL-BUILDING (measurements by volume)

1 Part Portland cement + 1 part lime + 5 parts of soft sand + water

or, if no lime is used:

1 part of Portland cement + 5 parts of soft sand + plasticizer + water.

Apart from plasticizers, there are other additives such as frost-proofing liquids, waterproofers and colourants. These colourants can be added to the cement before general mixing or added directly to the dry mix before water is added.

Where mortar will be visible, i.e. in the joints of walls or in the joints between paving slabs, it is important that it all ends up the same colour, whether or not a colourant is used. The only way of ensuring this is to measure out everything carefully in terms of volume, keeping a record of the exact mix in case some time has to elapse before the job can be completed.

MIXING

Mortar is mixed in a similar way to concrete, preferably on a large clean board so that no foreign bodies can get into the mix. Its consistency will depend upon its use. For walling, the mortar should be wet enough to stick to a vertical surface if thrown on to it, but not to the point where it will run afterwards. If it does not stick readily, it is probably too dry. A smooth, stiff creamy paste is one way of describing mortar for wall construction.

BUILDING A LOW BRICK WALL

This initial foray into bricklaying will be a half brick wall in stretcher bond (see page 34).

THE TOOLS

Straight edge and spirit level
Line and pins
Bricklayer's trowel and pointing trowel (Fig. 26)
Right angle square for corners
Club hammer ⎫
Bolster ⎬(Fig. 26)

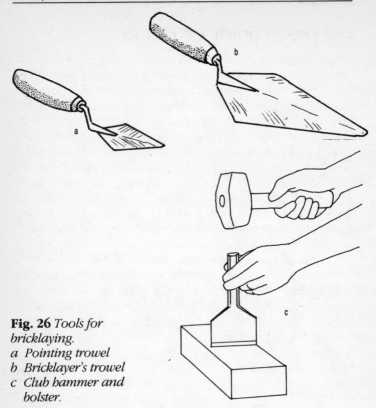

Fig. 26 *Tools for bricklaying.*
a Pointing trowel
b Bricklayer's trowel
c Club hammer and bolster.

Before starting it helps to load a small supply of mortar on a small 'spot' board and to stack a pile of bricks close by so that both are within easy reach of the work.

The foundation will be wider than the wall, so a line is needed to indicate exactly where the fair face of the wall is to be. This can be provided either by a scratch mark all along one side of the foundation or, better still, by a string line.

THE FIRST COURSE OF BRICKS

A line of mortar must be laid, using a trowel, down one length of the foundation, following the scratch or string line. Two bricks are then set exactly level upon the mortar bed, about the length of the straight edge apart (use a spirit level). One brick will probably represent one end or corner of the proposed wall. The other brick may well be only part way along (and temporary). By the time they have been tapped down into position, these bricks must be level in both planes and have squeezed out sufficient mortar to leave a full joint 1 cm (⅜ in) thick. If the joint ends up significantly less than this, there is probably insufficient mortar on the 'bed'. Keeping the quantity of mortar the same throughout the job is really the secret of success. If this varies, so will the joint thickness and the levels of the brickwork. If only mortar could be squeezed out of a tube like toothpaste, this particular aspect of the job would never be a problem! Bricks can be laid frog up or frog down. I prefer frog up.

Using a string line   Once these two initial bricks have been laid, a string can be stretched between, passing over the two opposite top fair face corners (Fig. 27). A 'tingle' of paper and a half-brick weight will help to hold the string in exactly the right position. Other bricks can be laid to the string, each one being tapped down until its top edge lines up precisely with the string. Each brick must also be level across. These bricks will also need a large blob of mortar on one end so that as each is brought down on to the mortar bed, it can be squeezed gently out against the previous brick, thus producing a 1 cm (⅜ in) thick vertical joint.

Extending the work   Once the bottom row of bricks has almost reached the 'temporary' brick, another

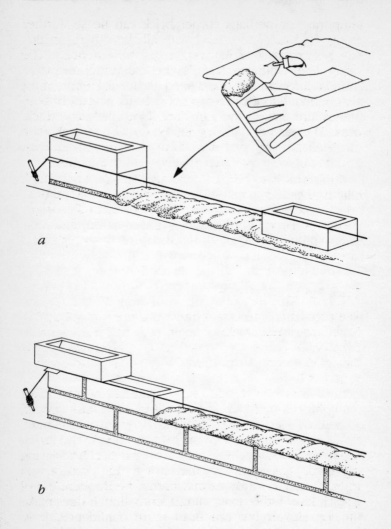

Fig. 27 *Laying bricks.*
a The first course of bricks
b The second course of bricks.

temporary or perhaps corner brick can be set further along the foundation, level with all the others, so that this bottom row of brickwork can be extended. The string line will also have to be extended so that a straight line can be maintained. A special effort must also be made to ensure that every brick is level in both planes and that all the joints are about the same thickness. The mortar which is squeezed out of each joint can be neatly trimmed off with the trowel and returned to the spot board or placed on top of the bricks.

If the wall is to be a certain exact length, a part brick may be needed to complete the length. This should be fitted in near the end but should never form the end or corner of a wall. You may feel, on reflection, that walls ought to be exactly half or whole bricks' long but this is not always possible.

THE NEXT COURSE

The second course is laid much like the first (Fig. 27b). It will, of course, have to begin with half a brick or, in the case of corners, a brick laid at right angles so that the bricks end up staggered or 'bonded' to form a stretcher bond.

In theory, it should not be necessary to have temporary intermediate bricks spanning this second course. As long as the end bricks are set on the same thickness of mortar, they ought to be level. The string can then be stretched between and the bricklaying resumed, governed by the string. In practice, an inexperienced bricklayer may prefer the frequent use of a spirit level rather than using a string line. It does make the job slower but can instil more confidence. It is, however, vital to try and regard brick laying as done in courses and not to focus too closely on each individual brick.

THE REST OF THE WALL

As the wall grows in height, particular care is needed to ensure that it remains perfectly vertical, both on its face and at the ends of corners. The vertical bubble on the spirit level is used for checking this.

Although most bricklayers have their own special way of working, it is well worthwhile watching a professional at work before embarking on the task yourself.

CUTTING BRICKS

Apart from using a disc cutter (angle grinder), the most effective technique is to place the brick on firm ground, place the blade of the bolster precisely where the cut is needed and strike its handle hard with the club hammer. This technique is ideal for half bricks but may not work so well where smaller portions of brick are required. In these cases, a disc cutter will be helpful but protective clothing, especially a face shield, must be worn.

MORTARED STONE WALLS

Any stone can be used but in colder areas soft sandstone will soon become mossy and break up after severe frosts. There are many different styles of stone walling and each requires a slightly different technique. All require a firm, preferably concrete foundation. Most free-standing stone walls will be quite thick if they are to have two fair faces. Many small stone garden walls retain soil and, therefore, require only one fair face. In some cases, however, the stone may not be thick enough to provide sufficient strength and will need a backing of concrete blocks. Where stone is reasonably thick a small retaining wall could be constructed in the following way.

SMALL STONE RETAINING WALL

Assuming that most of the stone is flattish – rather like thick paving stones and not all large square blocks, an attempt should be made to lay individual pieces as horizontally as possible. It helps to start with a level foundation.

A wide bed of mortar is laid along the foundation and a string line set up to indicate the front face of the wall. Since all the stones will be different thicknesses, the string cannot be used as a 'level' – only as a guide to ensure that the front of the wall is straight. It can sometimes be helpful to attach this string to two tall pegs set at either end of the wall in line with the front face. The line can then be moved up as the wall grows, thus providing a constant reference. A spirit level will also help to keep an upright wall perfectly vertical. Where the wall is to have a backward lean (a batter), these two pegs could be leaned back at the appropriate angle.

Vertical joints It is not always practical to apply mortar to the end of each stone before it is offered up to the one before (as is done with bricks). Once a row of stones has been laid, the joints between can be filled from above, although any excess mortar will have to be carefully removed from the front face. If weep holes are needed to allow the free drainage of water from behind the wall, these are best positioned near the base of the wall. They can be created by leaving out the mortar from some vertical joints. The wall, in this region, should be backfilled with some drainage aggregate.

Bonding and coursing Stones throughout the wall must span the joint below so that a bond is formed. A vertical joint running up through more than three layers of stone (Fig. 28) is a potential weakness and therefore

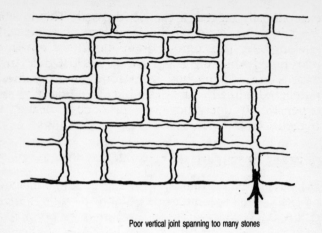

Poor vertical joint spanning too many stones

Fig. 28 *Random stone walling.*

bad practice. For this reason, stone must be carefully selected as work progresses.

Courses will tend to curve up and down, but where some stones are extra thick, two much thinner pieces may be used next to these in order to maintain some degree of coursing. Alternatively, some types of stone will split easily and can therefore be reduced in thickness.

All mortar joints, both horizontal and vertical, must be kept down as close to 1 cm (⅜ in) as possible. There is a great temptation to use mortar to make up levels in a stone wall. Particularly careful selection of stone will help to minimize this tendency.

As the wall nears its anticipated height, a serious attempt must be made to bring the last course level. This is not done by having excessively thick mortar joints, but by careful selection of stone thickness.

Dressed stone If the front face of any stone is

exceptionally ragged, it can be 'dressed'. This is where the edges are taken off the front face of stone with a pitching tool. The central part of the face is usually left untrimmed while the edges are cut back slightly, giving what is termed a 'pitched' face. Stone can sometimes be purchased already 'dressed' but it is usually more expensive. It does, however, produce a neater, less rugged looking wall.

A WALL WITH 'JUMPERS'

For stone which contains a number of large, rectangular blocks as well as flatter pieces, construction is slightly different. These large blocks are inserted every now and again, vertically spanning two or three courses (Fig. 28). They are often referred to as 'jumpers' and are featured in some types of manufactured or reconstituted stone walling. Because this type of stone is reasonably square, every attempt must be made to lay it as level as possible. With the more precise, manufactured units, this might be done with a spirit level. It is also possible to place mortar on the end of these blocks before offering them up to the ones already laid, as would be done in brickwork.

A WALL BACKED BY CONCRETE BLOCKS

The most likely thickness of concrete block used for this purpose is 100 mm (4 in). Coupled with the stone, it will mean having a concrete foundation width of at least 300 mm (12 in) × 2. Concrete blocks are laid like bricks using a line and pins, spirit level etc – a similar but more cumbersome process. The stone walling is built up at the same time and whenever the surface of a stone coincides with the surface of a concrete block, an expanded metal or a butterfly tie can be placed across the two, tying the two walls together. In brick walls

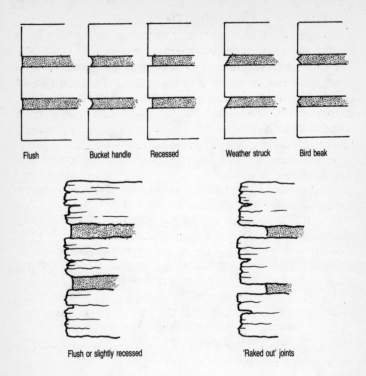

Flush   Bucket handle   Recessed   Weather struck   Bird beak

Flush or slightly recessed   'Raked out' joints

Fig. 29 *Styles of pointing.*

backed by blocks, this will occur every three rows of bricks but in stone walls it is much less predictable. The inevitable gaps or voids which are left in places between the blocks and the back of the stone work should be filled with mortar to produce a solid wall. This type of wall should always be built vertical, not with a batter (Fig. 14c). Near the top, the blockwork should give way to stone so that no concrete is visible above soil level in the raised bed.

POINTING

There are several different styles of pointing (Fig. 29). Most are carried out using a pointing trowel but various other tools can be used. The 'bucket handle' joint can, of course, be made with a piece of bucket handle but, more usually these days, a specially curved piece of metal is used. A recessed joint, whether it be in a wall or paving, is often made by drawing a square-edged piece of wood along a joint, leaving the mortar recessed and flat. Other devices can be used to 'rake out' or scrape out the mortar from between stones in a wall to make it look like a dry stone wall.

Pointing is usually carried out on the same day as construction before the mortar has completely set. If left too late the mortar becomes stiff and has to be cut or scraped into a style of pointing. If done too soon, the mortar may smear the face of the wall.

RENDERING

This is, in effect, a form of outdoor plastering which can be used to hide ugly concrete blocks and provide a smooth or textured surface for decorating with exterior masonry paint. Its more likely application on a patio is to provide a waterproof layer for the inside of a pool constructed from concrete blocks.

RENDERING THE INSIDE OF A POOL

The blocks (or bricks) must be clean and free from any loose material. Ideally, the joints should have been raked out to provide a key for the rendering. Rendering should never be done in hot sunshine and the blocks *must always be damp* – never dry.

The mixture used is one of sand and cement (plus a

plasticizer) but, unlike the mortar for walls, a clean (washed) graded or perhaps sharp sand is used. There are normally two coats. The first (undercoat) is about 8–12 mm (½–¾ in) thick and the second 5–8 mm (about ½ in) thick.

RECIPES FOR RENDERING A POOL

undercoat: 1 part cement with 4 parts sand + plasticizer

top coat: 1 part cement with 6 parts sand + plasticizer (or waterproofer)

Each coat can either be brushed on with an old broom head or be trowelled on with a float or plasterer's trowel. The mix must obviously be of a consistency which will facilitate one approach or the other. If the undercoat is trowelled on, the smooth finish should be scored in some way to provide a key for the top coat. The rendering must be prevented from drying out too quickly, otherwise it will crack. Once the undercoat has hardened (but before it actually dries) the top coat should be brushed or trowelled on leaving either a brushed or smooth finish. The top coat must also be allowed to cure slowly without drying out.

Rendering is a skill which needs practice. It is well worth practising on a piece of wall somewhere out of sight!

CHAPTER 5

LAYING PAVING

A SOUND BASE

In some areas, thin topsoil may conceal solid chalk, firm gravel or hoggin. In these cases, the topsoil can be removed and the paving laid directly onto a shaped base of this naturally compacted material. If drainage is poor, other better draining materials would have to be used.

Unless the ground is exceptionally unstable, in which case a raft of steel-reinforced concrete might be used, compacted hardcore or scalpings make an ideal base for most types of paving.

Hardcore is broken bricks and concrete. For patio work, relatively small pieces are best so that they can be compacted down to a fairly smooth surface. Whole or even half-bricks and similar size pieces of concrete are too lumpy.

Scalpings are a mixture of crushed rock and dust. The mixture of particle sizes gives a solid, compact base but ideally the largest pieces should not exceed 8 cm (3 in).

Geotechnic membrane is a fabric which can be laid on top of a soft excavation before the scalpings or hardcore are placed. It will prevent mud from oozing up through these materials and destabilizing them. It can also be used, under similar adverse conditions, to improve wheeled access to and from the work.

USEFUL TOOLS

rake
shovel
tamper
vibrating plate
club hammer
bolster
bricklayer's trowel and pointing trowel
spirit level
string line
straight edge

PLACING THE SCALPINGS

Assuming that a number of levelling pegs are protruding from the excavation, the scalpings or hardcore must be placed and compacted without disturbing them. In most cases, the peg tops will indicate the finished level of the paving and any falls across the area. The aim should be, therefore, to end up with scalpings the same distance down from the top of each peg, leaving enough room for the paving and its mortar (or sand).

COMPACTING

It is vital that the hardcore or scalpings base remains completely stable in all conditions and under whatever pressure may subsequently be exerted on it. For this reason it must be well compacted.

Tamper or punner This simple tool comprises a square steel block on the end of a steel shaft. It is repeatedly thrust down on to the hardcore or scalpings until the material has been sufficiently compacted.

Vibrating plate   A mechanical device, usually powered by a petrol engine, which has a steel plate that vibrates and thus compacts most materials very efficiently. The tool is very heavy but the mechanism is arranged so that the vibration actually drives the device slowly forwards, making it surprisingly light and easy to operate. For large areas, it is well worth hiring one of these machines rather than depending on a tamper.

MORTAR

A typical mix for mortar beneath paving, more especially slabs, would be: 1 part cement to 5 parts of soft sand (plus, perhaps, a plasticizer).

Its consistency should be such that it is wet enough to stick to the paving but just firm enough to support its weight. If the mortar is too stiff or too wet neither of these two functions will be possible. Gentle tapping of the slab with a club hammer and piece of wood should then produce a good response.

CUTTING

A disc cutter or angle grinder, already mentioned under brick cutting, can also be very useful for slabs. It may not always be practical to cut all the way through but a deep scoring will, in many cases, be enough to enable the slab to be finally cut through with a club hammer and bolster. Using a club hammer and bolster for the entire job can be tricky but was, of course, the main technique used before the days of powered tools.

USE OF CLUB HAMMER AND BOLSTER

The method I have found useful is as follows. The slab is marked with a chalk line and stood on edge so that this

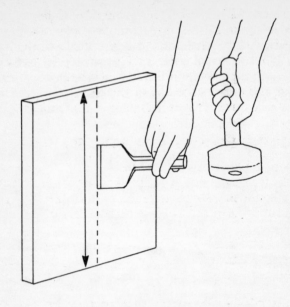

Fig. 30 *Cutting a slab with a club hammer and bolster.*

mark is vertical (Fig. 30). The vertical slab is supported by either your left or right leg and heel so that the entire length of the chalk line has some support behind. The club hammer and bolster are used, not too violently, up and down the chalk line so that a shallow groove is gradually cut. Only two or three knocks are needed in any one spot before moving up or down to the next. Eventually, patience should be rewarded by a tell-tale change in the sound which the bolster makes – from a high pitched 'chink' to a much lower tone. This usually heralds the long awaited cut – hopefully in the right place! The thicker, pressed slabs often cut better than cheaper thinner ones although they do take longer. Unfortunately the cut edge is often quite rough, not like the smooth finish left by a cutting disc. If this technique fails it could be because your leg was not lined up exactly with the chalk line. It is also vital that the back of the slab is in actual contact with your leg for as much of its length as possible. It is this which helps to absorb the shock and prevent the line of weakness from straying off the chalk mark. Protect your legs with trousers.

CUTTING BLOCKS AND PAVIORS

Concrete block paviors can be cut in the same way as bricks (see page 60). A hydraulic cutter is also available from some hire shops. It works by squeezing the blocks into submission but is less effective on slabs.

With the foundation compacted into position, the level pegs set to the right falls and all the tools and materials at the ready, a start can be made on laying the paving.

LAYING SLABS USING THE 'SPOT' TECHNIQUE

If the area to be paved has one side up against a building, it is likely that this particular side will be laid level, perhaps in line with some existing brickwork. There should already be some pegs indicating this. A string line should be stretched tightly across here, from one side to the other so that slabs can be laid to the line. Even if the paving is not against a building, there is still likely to be one side which has to be set out level. Since slabs are rarely laid level in both directions it is almost certain that an adjacent side has been given a fall. A string line is needed along here too, just skirting the peg tops and indicating the line along which the slabs will be laid. This second string line will often be at 90° to the first (especially where square slabs are being used).

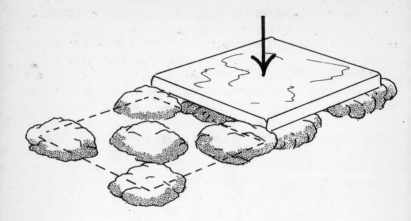

Fig. 31 *Spot bedding for slabs.*

THE FIRST SLABS

The best way to hold a slab ready for laying is by two diagonally opposite corners. Five reasonably generous blobs or spots of mortar are put down, in the corners and centres so that a slab can rest on them (Fig. 31). A slab is offered up carefully and allowed to rest on the mortar which should give, just a little, under the weight. At this point, the surface of the slab must still be well above the string line (perhaps by the thickness of the slab). It must also be lined up with the two strings. Using a club hammer on a small piece of wood, the slab can be gently banged down so that eventually the two top outer edges line up precisely with the strings. The slab should then be level in one direction and have a predetermined fall in the other. A spirit level can be used to keep an eye on the levels.

By the time the slab has been banged down to the string lines, the spots of mortar should have just about merged into a solid bed beneath the slab. If there are still large voids between the spots, not enough mortar was put down in the first place. If banging down has to become violent and persistent before the string lines are eventually reached, then too much mortar has been used or the mortar was too dry. Excessively wet mortar will obviously just collapse under the weight of the slab.

A similar process is followed for the next slab. If, for example, a slab along the sloping string is laid next, it will have to line up with the string for its correct fall but will also have to line up with the previous slab which, in that direction, will be level. As the slab is gently banged down into position, both the string line and the edge of the adjacent slab will have to be watched. At the same time a joint can be left between the two slabs.

Although it is possible to judge by eye when two adjacent slabs are at precisely the same level, feeling the two edges under the palm of your hand can also be a very good way of testing the levels especially if your palm is resting across the join while the slabs are being given any final, fine adjustment.

Joints The width of joints can be controlled by small wedges or pieces of wood 7–10 mm (¼ in) thick. These can be used throughout the job, being removed once the bed has set. Some variation is bound to occur if the slabs have a rustic edge.

WORKING OUT FROM THE CORNER

The first two rows of slabs really decide the levels for all the rest but, like passing a message down a long line of command, there is a danger that as work progresses, the levels could be lost, especially if the slabs are twisted or riven. For this reason, a spirit level and straight edge should never be far away. Hopefully there will also be some level pegs accurately set out which can be used as a further check throughout the job. It is also a good idea to stand back and look at the job as it progresses – the eye can often detect a problem that was missed close to.

At this point, it is worth reflecting on what would happen if the compacted base (and the pegs) had not been put in at the correct levels. If, for example, the whole base had been put in level then, in order to achieve a fall, some slabs would have to be on a much thicker mortar bed than others. Slab laying is considerably more difficult if the amount of mortar beneath is constantly having to be revised.

POINTING

Pointing should only be done when the mortar beneath the slabs is set and the slabs are dry.

MORTAR FOR POINTING

Sharp sand, rather than soft builders' sand should be used for pointing. Proportions can be the same as for brick work mortar (see page 54), although a plasticizer is not really appropriate. On the other hand, a colourant might be needed.

The mix should be less wet than before so that it does not smear the surface of the paving. For this reason, it is better not to point paving if its surface is wet. A dusting of fine, dry sand before pointing can help to reduce smearing and staining.

POINTING STYLES

There are a number of pointing styles, mostly similar to those used in walls. Flush pointing is also used where the mortar is cut off flush with the surface of the paving. In some circumstances, especially with old stone paving, pointing can be omitted and the joints filled with sand or fine soil. As long as these joints link up with some porous material beneath the slabs, thyme and other carpeting plants can be encouraged to populate the paving. Unfortunately, weeds will also grow and have to be removed by hand.

QUICK POINTING

There is a popular misconception that a dry mix of sand and cement, if swept into the joints and watered afterwards, will form a hard and durable joint. It has been my experience that if the sand and cement are very dry, the water does not penetrate properly. Although the normal method of pointing involves the use of a pointing trowel, it is possible to sweep in a damp mix, compact it in some way and then to water it. This will produce better results than the dry approach. Most paving projects will include the need to cut some slabs or blocks.

LAYING SLABS USING THE FULL BED METHOD

There are different interpretations of this method. Some might argue that, if done properly, the spot method should end up as a full bed! One of the easiest techniques is to make sure that the compacted base is as near to the desired levels and falls as possible. It will also be better done in scalpings rather than hardcore, because a semi-dry mix of sand and cement will be raked out over the base and with hardcore, there is a danger that this would be lost between the pieces of hardcore.

The proportion of cement to sand for the full bed is likely to be as follows: 1 part of cement to about 8 parts of soft sand. The sand should be damp (not wet), so that the mixture can give a degree of compaction and adhesion yet be raked.

SCREEDING

An even thickness of about 30 mm (1¼ in) is raked out (screeded) over the base so that, if possible, it is perfectly smooth and to the right levels. Only a limited area can be done at any one time since the screed must not be trodden on. The final levelling of this mix can be done with a strip of wood or narrow screed board (perhaps 25 × 100 mm or 1 × 4 in). The slabs are then laid carefully on this bed and gently tapped down, although there will not be much flexibility for any adjustment. There will probably be no string lines representing the levels but, hopefully, some pegs from the setting-out stage. Evenly spaced joints are once again formed with the help of wooden spacers.

This full bed technique is not really suited to slabs or pieces of stone which vary in thickness, nor is it suitable for thin, fragile slabs, especially if they are twisted.

BRICK PAVING

With bricks as small as they are, the spot bed technique is hardly appropriate. If stock bricks are used, they are likely to be too uneven for the full bed technique either, so a compromise between the two is more usually adopted.

PREPARING A MORTAR BED

Make up a wet mortar mix similar to that used under slabs (page 75). Ideally, this should be put down with a shovel and spread to form a bed about 35 mm (1½ in) thick. It is then chopped up a little into peaks and troughs so that when bricks are laid upon it, there is some flexibility.

LAYING THE BRICKS

Bricks are set out in whatever pattern has been chosen and small joints left between them so that the pattern fits exactly both ways. The width of these joints will depend upon the dimensions of the particular bricks chosen. A whole patch, perhaps a square metre or yard, can be laid out before the bricks are collectively and gently tapped down to the appropriate levels with a club hammer on a long piece of wood (about 1.2 m or 4 ft long).

As with slabs, it will have been helpful if the compacted base has been laid to the correct levels and the mortar spread to a fairly even thickness. This first patch of brick paving should end up level in one direction and with an appropriate fall in the other. The process is repeated until the whole area is complete. If the bricks are dry and dusty, they should be brushed off and dampened before they are laid but must not be pointed up until their surface is reasonably dry.

HAUNCHING

The bricks around the edge will be particularly vulnerable to damage and need some protection. This is achieved by building up mortar all around the outside edges so that it slopes up towards the top outside edge at about 45°. This mortar is usually brought to within 25 mm (1 in) of the top of each brick. Any higher, and it would be visible above the soil in any adjacent border. It is very important that the compacted base material extends a little way beyond the paving so that this haunching can sit on a proper base and not be hanging on to the side of the bricks with no firm support below (Fig. 32). All types of paving and kerbing should be haunched around the outside edges to prevent damage and subsidence.

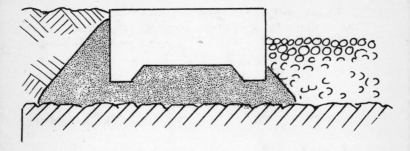

Fig. 32 *Brick edging haunched on the outside.*

BRICK AND BLOCK PAVIORS

There are two slightly different techniques for both based on the same general principles. The one described here, called the sand bed technique, is most applicable to larger areas of paving, even driveways. The variation described in Chapter 6 applies much more to garden paths.

Brick and block paviors are usually laid on a sand bed then vibrated down to a point where they will not subside any further even when a heavy weight, like a vehicle, is applied to their surface.

The area to be paved will, like any other form of paving, require a base of compacted materials (preferably scalpings) laid to the correct levels. In addition, a very secure edging is needed all round the area.

EDGING

Where the paving comes up against a building then, of course, this can act as the edging. Elsewhere, a very

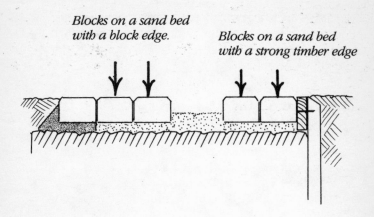

Fig. 33 *Examples of edging for paviors.*

stout and well-supported timber edge or, better still, a well haunched brick or block edge should be installed (Fig. 33). For the latter, the compacted base must be sufficiently extended to support both an edging and generous haunching. There must be no haunching on the inside of the edging – any excess mortar should be cut off flush with the side of the paviors. In terms of design, the edging of blocks-bricks will either match or contrast with the main materials.

A FLUSH FINISH

Around driveways the edge may have to be proud of the paved area to form a kerb, but in many instances the intention will be to have the main area flush with the edging. To achieve this the work should continue as follows. A bed of sharp sand is spread over a reasonable area, bearing in mind that it must not be trodden on. It is usually raked out, then screeded and very gently compacted with a strip of wood or a straight edge so that it ends up exactly the right level and *just* firm. Its surface can then be very lightly raked to produce a slight tilth or roughness.

Depth of sand The most critical question is how far up the edging this sand should be brought so that once the blocks have been placed upon it and vibrated down, complete compaction and a flush finish coincide. The moisture content of sand is variable and this, in turn, decides the degree of compaction possible. In any event, the sand must be damp – *not dry*. The degree of compaction will also depend upon the weight of the vibrating plate. As a rule of thumb, the paviors, when placed on the prepared, non-vibrated sand base, should protrude above the top surface of the edging by about 15 mm (⅝ in), seldom more. A small trial area should be vibrated down just to see if, for that particular sand and vibrating plate, the distance is right. In some circumstances the sand and paviors may go down only 5 mm (¼ in). It must be stressed that the edging will come under considerable stress during the vibration process so any concrete or mortar used for these edges must be well set and strong.

PLACING THE PAVIORS

Once a good-sized area of sand has been prepared to the appropriate levels, the paviors can be placed out in whatever pattern is required. No gap is left between them – they must be butted tightly up to one another. Hopefully, the fixed edges will have been positioned to allow an exact number of paviors to be fitted in, otherwise some tricky cutting could be necessary.

USING A VIBRATING PLATE

A vibrating plate, preferably fitted with a protective rubber mat (to prevent scratching), is then used over the area until the paviors end up flush with the edges and to smooth levels. The vibrating plate must not, however, be allowed to come too close to any open ended paviors (where laying is to be continued) for fear of causing subsidence and a general disintegration of the pattern. Any area affected in this way must have its sand re-laid.

It cannot be overstressed that, before vibration takes place, all the paviors are fitted tightly between fixed edges, so that sideways movement cannot occur. Any slackness will mean that during vibration paviors will tend to move and straight lines within any pattern will be disrupted.

Once all the blocks have been vibrated into position, a dressing of dry silver sand can be spread over the surface and swept into the cracks. If there is a choice of vibrating plate on hire, use the heavier model for driveways or a lighter version for patios where vehicular traffic is not expected.

OTHER DECORATIVE FILLINGS

BRICK/BLOCK INFILLING

If the paving design is a mix of brick and slabs, it must be remembered that bricks are often thicker than slabs and will therefore need less mortar beneath them if they are to end up at the same level. The other point to bear in mind is that 600 mm (24 in) slabs are not as compatible with bricks as 450 mm (18 in) slabs, because the measurements of a brick, especially the length or width, fit neatly into units measuring 450 mm, 900 mm and so on. This will need considering at the design stage, otherwise there could be a lot of brick cutting later.

CONCRETE PAVING WITH A BRICK EDGE

Although plain concrete usually looks unattractive and is reserved mainly for utilitarian purposes, there is at least one way of making concrete look more attractive – perhaps where it has been used for a washing line area, dustbin enclosure or a ramp.

EXPOSED AGGREGATE CONCRETE

Assuming that the concrete will not need to support vehicular traffic, a compacted base of hardcore (or scalpings) can be used. A brick edge may then be mortared all around the outside and haunched. Once this has set, thin polythene sheeting is draped over these edges to protect them from subsequent concreting. This concrete must be *batch* mixed to something like: 1 part cement to 6 parts all-in ballast + 1 or 2 parts 5 mm or 10 mm shingle.

It is laid and tamped over the area, ending up flush with the edges. It is obviously vital to ensure that the edging reflects the overall levels and falls. Tamping is normally done with the tamping board spanning across and resting on the edges but this often leaves ridges which will need smoothing or floating off with a float – a large rectangular trowel. If this concreting is done on a cloudy or humid day, a polythene covering is not, initially, needed.

After about six hours (a little longer in cool weather) the surface of the concrete can be *very gently* hosed down and brushed clean with a soft broom. This will remove cement from the very surface to expose the aggregate (including the additional shingle). The edging bricks are protected by the polythene (part of which will be trapped beneath the concrete). Over washing will loosen stones and begin to erode the actual surface. Once the washing has been carried out, the concrete must then be protected with polythene and left to cure.

In a day or two, this polythene can be removed and the thin polythene covering the edges cut away. There might be a slight 'bloom' or haze still covering the exposed stones. This will be a thin cement deposit which can be cleaned off with a proprietary masonry cleaner (acid wash). The concrete must be completely set before this is used and it should be remembered that this acid wash could damage plants or grass and temporarily taint soil.

An even more attractive finish can be achieved in the following way. The edges are fixed and protected as before. An ordinary concrete mix (1:6) is used (without the additional shingle) to within, say, 20 mm (¾ in) of the top of the edging. This last 20 mm can then be filled with a special mix of cement and aggregate. The aggregate could be granite chippings, or shingle or whatever would look attractive once exposed. It does help to have a mixture of stone sizes so that the mix has some strength and interest although, in reality, it is only a veneer. This is then washed and exposed in the same way as before. Batching is essential to ensure an even result right across the whole area. Large areas should be concreted in alternating bays so that expansion joints can be incorporated as work progresses. This will help to stop indiscriminate cracking.

CHAPTER 6

GARDEN PATHS

Many paths do, of course, feature the materials already discussed but often in a slightly different way. There are also other materials which are used more commonly for paths than they are for patios. Since paths are obviously highly functional, their width and the route they take need careful consideration. You will almost certainly live with the result for a long time.

DESIGNING A PATH

ITS ROUTE

A path from the street to the main entrance will probably be the busiest, with its use being more essential than leisurely. It should, therefore, be reasonably direct. The postman, for example, will not have time for tricky manoeuvring and, if pressed, will cut across flower beds and lawns rather than follow the path. These direct routes are called 'desire lines'. The path has either to take these lines of least resistance (within reason) or, if not direct, have certain features (e.g. prickly bushes!) to prevent short cuts.

In an ornamental area of the garden a more indirect and interesting route is usually more appropriate because the circumstances are mainly leisurely and the idea is to give access to different sections.

WIDTH

The main path from the street must be wide enough to cope with two or more people wishing to pass in opposite directions. Near the main door an even wider area of path could be useful for visitors waiting to be invited in, so that they can stand together without having to form a queue down the path. These main paths should be at least 1 m (3 ft 3 in) wide, preferably more. If they are lengthy, a wider point part way along would be useful for people to pass each other comfortably.

Paths which are likely to be used by only one person at a time (e.g. to the dustbin, compost heap, garden seat etc) should still be at least 60 cm (24 in) wide. Paths narrower than this are useful for only occasional access. Those which cross or border lawns should be flush with or fractionally below grass level so that a mower can pass over the edge and cut all the grass. If this is not possible, a narrow border or a mowing strip (devoid of grass) along the path edge will help to simplify mowing.

SETTING OUT

If the path is to have several curves across, say, a lawn, and there is no plan on paper, its route will have to be drawn on the ground. The best technique is to draw with a thin line of sand or humus which shows up particularly well on grass. If the first attempt needs adjusting, the line can easily be rubbed out with a broom and re-drawn.

The surface of the path, like previous examples of paving, will need predicting and controlling with pegs. Where the path crosses an existing lawn, its level will probably, as already explained, need to be guided by the surface of the grass. If however, the surrounding garden has yet to be developed, the level of the path could be decided independently. Where the path has to begin and end at certain fixed levels and take a smooth (non-undulating) route between these two points, three 'boning rods' can be very useful.

Boning rods These are made from two pieces of wood fitted together in the form of a T. The cross bar usually measures about 60 mm (24 in) and the vertical bar perhaps 1.2 m (4 ft). Boning rods are nearly always used in threes and their use is made easier by painting the cross bars black with a white strip (about 1 cm or 3/8 in deep). along the top edge. All three rods must be the same size.

One is stood or held upright at one fixed end of the path and another at the furthest end. The third is held upright, anywhere along the line of the proposed path. By standing at one end and looking across the horizontal bar to the boning rod at the far end, it is easy to see if the intermediate rod is too high or low. When all three tops line up with each other, the rods are obviously all on the same level. The only rod that should be adjusted up or down to achieve this is the intermediate one, not the fixed ends. By working between these two ends along the proposed line of the path, pegs can be inserted underneath the intermediate boning rod, so that eventually, all their tops reflect what can be best described as a 'running' level.

Winding paths The boning rods can be used in the same way for a winding path. The observer at one end, merely moves a little in relation to the boning rods so that their tops still appear to coincide, at least for part of their width. It would be usual to set out just one side of the path in this way, then decide whether the opposite side should be level, lower or higher. This opposite row of pegs can be put in with the help of a straight edge and spirit level coming across from the first row of pegs.

THE DEPTH OF EXCAVATION

This is decided and controlled in the same way as described for more general areas of paving. If a path should cross an area where there are isolated concentrations of exceptionally deep or soft topsoil, excavation will have to go deeper just here and extra hardcore or scalpings put in. Where a path is to have a brick, block or concrete edge, the base or foundation should be extended out to support this.

EDGINGS

Paths made from loose or mobile materials need some form of edging. Some other types of paths may also be given an edging, if only for aesthetic reasons.

TIMBER

This is relatively inexpensive and easy to install. The sawn timber usually used is in the form of long strips about 75–100 mm (3–4 in) wide and 15–25 mm (¾–1 in) thick. Pegs are also needed, about 35–50 mm (1½–2 in) square and long enough to extend down into firm ground. Their frequency will depend upon the thickness and stability of the side strips and how many bends or joins are necessary. On average pegs will be needed every 1.2 m (4 ft). If timber edging is anticipated at the setting out stage, the level pegs could double up as the support pegs, with the timber edging being fixed directly to these, flush with their tops, after excavation. All timber must have been pressure treated to resist decay.

If grass is to be brought right up to the timber edge, the most effective results are achieved by making the compacted, prepared soil flush with the timber edging, then laying turf right over the top of it (Fig. 34a).

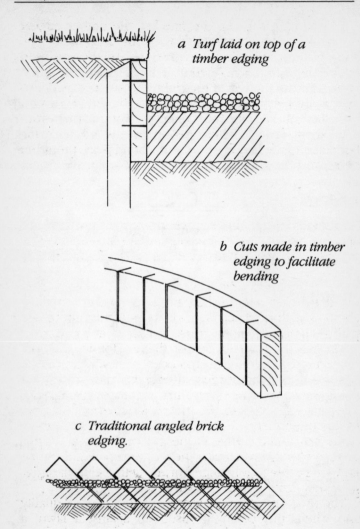

a Turf laid on top of a
  timber edging

b Cuts made in timber
  edging to facilitate
  bending

c Traditional angled brick
  edging.

Fig. 34 *Examples of edging for paths.*

If pronounced bends are needed, the timber edging can be cut half way through every 5 cm (2 in) or so (Fig. 34b), making sure that these saw cuts are always closed up by the bend, not opened. Obviously, as the bend switches from the left to the right, the saw cuts will also have to be switched from one side of the timber strip to the other. All saw cuts must receive extra treatment with a wood preservative. These edging strips would normally be nailed to the inside of the supporting pegs, but some bends may need extra pegs on the opposite side too.

BRICKS

In addition to the brick edging already described for areas of paving, a traditional technique of setting bricks on end at an angle of about 45° can also be useful (Fig. 34c)

A narrow trench about 65 mm (2½ in) wide is taken out down each side of the path, deep enough to allow about one third of each brick to protrude above the path's surface. The first brick is laid in at the correct angle then others laid against this in domino fashion. Once a reasonable length has been laid out, soil can be brought in on the outside and whatever base material is being used, brought up against the inside. Both sides are compacted, taking care not to knock the bricks out of line (a punner or tamper is useful on a job like this). Since it is unlikely that all the top corners will, at this stage, be level, a reasonably heavy piece of wood can be laid across them and banged firmly with a club hammer until they have all gone down evenly.

The bricks must be of an engineering or stock quality and where this edging is used up against a lawn, a mowing strip will be needed. This type of edging is normally used in conjunction with gravel or shingle paths. No concrete is necessary unless the edge has to be especially strong.

CONCRETE

Although used mainly around driveways, this edging might, in some situations, prove useful for garden paths. Two main styles are available – square topped or round topped. Most are in lengths of about 60–90 cm (2–3 ft) and 15 cm (6 in) wide. This limited width means that there is insufficient merely to be held in position with compacted earth – concrete has to be used along with fairly generous haunching on the outside. A string line helps to strike a smooth level but problems can arise on curves. Only gentle curves are possible with whole kerbs. Tighter curves require smaller portions, and even then, results may not be particularly smooth. These kerbs are usually used in conjunction with gravels and shingles which would normally finish about 35 mm (1½ in) down from the kerb top.

ROPE TILES

These Victorian edging tiles (and their modern equivalents) come in a variety of styles and colours. They are quite deep and can, therefore, be put into the ground without any concrete or haunching (unless the ground is particularly soft). They do not provide a good edge to a lawn because of their susceptibility to the physical damage inflicted by lawn mowers. They are most appropriate separating shingle from soil. A shingle path running between a lawn and a border might, for example, have a concealed timber edge alongside the lawn and rope tiles alongside the border.

DRAINAGE

The presence of kerbs or edgings may create a drainage problem, particularly if the path itself is below general ground level.

Water is more likely to drain away into border soil than it is into compacted lawn so, wherever appropriate, a path could be given a cross fall towards a border. In addition, gaps should be left in the lower kerb so that water can escape. Where a path is made up from shingle or gravel over scalpings, water should soak away quite efficiently but, if beneath these, there is heavy clay, a problem could eventually arise.

PATH MATERIALS

SHINGLE

The rounded stones of shingle mean that it will not compact and will always be on the move. It must, therefore, be contained with edging and, if possible, be kept well below the top of the edging. Several stone sizes are available, the most common being 5 mm and 10 mm. The layer of shingle should never be more than about three stones deep, raked out over a firm base, perhaps hoggin.

HOGGIN

This material is a natural mixture of round stones, sand and clay.The proportion of these and the size of stones will vary according to where it has been dug and, for paths, hoggin with relatively small stones is needed. Kerbs or edgings and a well compacted base are needed to contain and support about 35–50 mm (1½–2 in) of compacted hoggin.

The hoggin is placed and raked out over the compacted base then rolled or vibrated hard. A vibrating roller or vibrating plate would normally be used but a roller has to be kept wet so that the hoggin does not stick to it. However, it must be stressed that too much water will result in disaster with the hoggin becoming too soft and almost impossible to compact properly. Although the degree of compaction will obviously depend upon moisture content, stone size and so on, it can usually be assumed that if the uncompacted hoggin is raked out almost flush with the edging tops, compaction will take it down by at least 20–30 mm (¾–1¼ in).

Immediately after compaction the hoggin will look rather unattractive but by the time rain has washed it several times a clean, attractive pebbly surface should have been exposed. Hoggin is usually a golden brown or a slightly reddish sandy colour. Once compacted, it is not very porous and if its surface is poorly drained, the overall effect can be spoiled by an accumulation of sticky silt which, in time, will support moss and weeds. Its surface can be further enhanced by a *thin* layer of similarly coloured shingle with a pebble size of between 5 and 10 mm.

PATH GRAVEL

In contrast to shingle which has rounded stones and will not compact, path gravel is a mixture of tiny angular pieces of stone and dust which will compact to give a hard but slightly gravelly surface. Like hoggin, path gravel needs a firm edge and a compact (preferably well-drained) base. Because there are no stones as such, it can be put down as a relatively thin layer, say 25–35 mm (1–1½ in) after compaction. For successful compaction gravel must be damp – not dry, but never wet. A vibrating plate or roller is used. Its surface may be semi-porous but good surface drainage is still very important. There is quite a wide range of colours available, mainly from grey, through brown to rusty red. A slightly different grade is often used for driveways and areas of heavy use.

BRICKS AND BLOCKS

Techniques for laying these materials already described in Chapter 5 still apply, but compaction without the use of a vibrating plate could be considered since a garden path may not need to support heavy weights. Once the bricks or blocks have been laid out on the sand bed, a heavy strip of timber (perhaps 75 × 75 mm or 3 in square) can be laid across and hit firmly with a heavy club hammer. This process is repeated in a strictly systematic fashion until, gradually, the units have been compacted down as far as they will go. The depth of the sand bed should then be re-assessed so that, after compaction, the bricks or blocks end up at the appropriate level in relation to the edging, whether flush or recessed.

WOOD/BARK CHIPS

In a woodland garden, a path with timber edging and bark chippings often looks highly attractive and, in time, its surface can be boosted with additional chippings.

The edging can either be sawn and pegged timber or a more rustic effect, using straight or gently curving branches. Ideally, peeled and tanalized poles should be used for durability but a curve may then have to be created from short, straight lengths. Branches of birch (*Betula*) decay far too quickly but oak (*Quercus robur*) is particularly durable, though rarely straight. Sweet chestnut (*Castanea sativa*) is also very durable. Compacted soil – perhaps using a vibrating plate – is an adequate base. Very sandy soil with a low percentage of humus could have some cement raked in before compaction for extra stability. The chippings are then spread over the compacted base to a depth of about 35 mm (1½ in), not too much more. Some bark chippings do release a brown stain when they are first wetted but this diminishes in time.

PATH MATERIALS

	Advantages	Disadvantages
Hoggin	Firm surface Suitable for heavy use Mellow colouring	Can be difficult to lay May become sticky Relatively expensive
Shingle	Easy to lay Relatively inexpensive Mellow colouring Noisy – good for security	Mobile, especially on a slope Needs a firm base Difficult to remove leaves etc.
Path gravels	Attractive/mellow colours Fairly stable and firm Relatively easy to clean	Relatively expensive Quite difficult to lay Needs good surface drainage May become sticky
Brick and block paviors	Hard wearing Attractive colours Choice of patterns	Relatively expensive Needs a good base Curves are a little more difficult to achieve than with other materials
Concrete	Long lasting Easy to clean	Heavy work to install Relatively expensive Not particularly attractive
Wood/ bark chips	Attractive Soft, ideal in a woodland garden	Need some sort of base Very mobile Can stain Difficult to remove leaves completely Eventual decay

INDEX

Page numbers in *italic* refer to the illustrations